CLASSIC WISDOM

TODAY'S QUESTIONS. TIMELESS ANSWERS.

Looking for time-tested guidance for the dilemmas of the spiritual life? Find it in the company of the wise spiritual masters of our Catholic tradition.

Forthcoming volumes will include wisdom from:
Francis de Sales
James Alberione
Luis Martinez

2013

Strength in Darkness

CLASSIC WISDOM COLLECTION

Strength in Darkness

Wisdom from John of the Cross

Compiled and with a Foreword
by Margaret Kerry, FSP

Pauline
BOOKS & MEDIA
Boston

Library of Congress Cataloging-in-Publication Data

John of the Cross, Saint, 1542–1591.
 [Selections. English. 2011]
 Strength in darkness : wisdom from John of the Cross / compiled and with a foreword by Margaret Kerry.
     p. cm. -- (Classic wisdom collection).
 ISBN 0-8198-7139-7 (pbk.)
 1. Spiritual life—Catholic Church. I. Kerry, Margaret Charles, 1957– II. Title.
 BX2179.J63 2011
 248.2'2—dc22

2010031641

The Scripture quotations contained in the foreword are from the *New Revised Standard Version Bible: Catholic Edition*, copyright © 1989, 1993, Division of Christian Education of the National Council of the Churches of Christ in the United States of America. Used by permission. All rights reserved.

From *The Collected Works of St. John of the Cross*, translated by Kieran Kavanaugh and Otilio Rodriguez, copyright © 1964, 1979, 1991 by Washington Province of Discalced Carmelites ICS Publications 2131 Lincoln Road, N.E. Washington, DC 20002-1199 U.S.A. www.icspublications.org.

Cover design by Rosana Usselmann

Cover photo by Mary Lou Winters, FSP

Published by Pauline Books & Media, 50 Saint Pauls Avenue, Boston, MA 02130-3491. www.pauline.org.

Printed in the U.S.A.

Pauline Books & Media is the publishing house of the Daughters of St. Paul, an international congregation of women religious serving the Church with the communications media.

1 2 3 4 5 6 7 8 9   15 14 13 12 11

Dedicated to companions

on the journey of "going through."

May you know the

"secret and peaceful and loving inflow of God."

Contents

Foreword

Have you ever had that abiding sense that you just can't get through something? Things that you could have walked away from at one time now settle in the pit of your stomach. Traumatic losses take away what equilibrium you had. Someone you love dies. Losing a job challenges who you are and the meaning of your life. A failed relationship leaves you wounded and heartbroken.

Faith is tested in this suffering. Our anger rages against those we love, against God. We panic. We want to run away but don't know where. Who will love us in this condition? The one thing we do know is that we don't want to endure the pain. We are ready to accept anything that offers a promise of release from the difficult path of self-transcendence. How are we to believe that God heals in this night? Can emptiness, fear, and pain really enkindle a "flame of love"?

One year after the death of my father, while still grieving, I transferred to a new community. The loss of two roles came with this move. I found myself in an unexpected crisis. The meaning that life held was sucked out of me. I didn't know whom to turn to or where to go. I was unable to make sense of these upheavals. My spiritual life was in crisis. I no longer had any feelings during prayer. John of the Cross expressed what I felt so well: *nada, nada, nada* (nothing, nothing, nothing).

I found insight and enlightenment in ordinary road signs: When a sign read, "Dangerous intersection ahead," my prayer became, "Hide me in the shelter of your wings!" For "Blind driveway," I prayed, "Lord, open my eyes!" "No driving in the breakdown lane" became "Drive slowly in the breakdown lane." "Yield" became "Stay where you are," "Go slow," and "Yield to God." On a neighborhood street, "Go slow, children" reminded me, "I am a child in all of this and in need of you."

Pseudo-Dionysus, an early Christian thinker, wrote: "In the dark night of the Cross all the greatness of divine love appears: where reason no longer sees, love does."[1] Saint John of the Cross understood what this fifth-century theologian meant. When we find ourselves entering a crisis of faith, hovering on the edge of hope, we have received an invitation to go deeper. John encourages us not to walk away from but to go through whatever it is we face, because in the final analysis it will lead us to freedom in love. This purified love will be greater and stronger than anything we have encountered. John describes this as a time God gently and lovingly awakens in our heart as we enter an unknown land and travel unknown roads. John echoes Isaiah: "I will lead the blind by a road they do not know, by paths they have not known I will guide them. I will turn the darkness before them into light, the rough places into level ground. These are the things I will do, and I will not forsake them" (Isa 42:16).

Juan de Yepes y Álvarez was born in a small town not far from Avila, Spain, in 1542. His father, Gonzalo de Yepes, was from a family of wealthy silk merchants. Gonzalo's family disinherited him when he married Catalina Álvarez, a weaver from an unprivileged background. Their love joyfully welcomed three sons, Francisco, Luis, and John. When John was still a child, his brother Luis died, followed shortly by his father. Catalina Álvarez struggled to support

Francisco and John. She sent John for elementary studies as an apprentice to a local carpenter and stonemason. At the age of seventeen John went to care for the sick at a hospital for the poor in Medina. He nursed patients with the plague or other contagious diseases while also collecting alms to support the work. While in Medina, John enrolled in a nearby Jesuit college. By the time he was twenty he was attracted to the contemplative spirit of the Carmelite Order. Without hesitation he joined, receiving the name John of Saint Matthias. After completing studies at the renowned University of Salamanca, he was ordained a priest in 1567.

John knew what success felt like. He had been prefect of studies. His projects had gone smoothly, and the Order entrusted him with positions of leadership. It was not long after his ordination that young John met the wise Teresa of Ávila. She had heard that John was looking for an even more rigorous way of life, and she invited him to join her reform of Carmel. After their first meeting, Saint Teresa hurried to tell her sisters: "Help me, daughters, to give thanks to our Lord God, for we already have a friar and a half to begin the reform of the Friars."[2] Antonio de Heredia was the "full" friar, while John was the "half." Later, she wrote: "He is not tall, but I think he is of great stature in God's eyes." Saint Teresa probably referred to the young friar's eloquent reflections on love between God and the soul as well as his ability to pitch in to help the nuns put up walls, hang doors, and fix leaky ceilings.

Resistance against the reform, however, was building in his former community, and in 1575 the General Chapter of the Order suppressed monasteries of the reform. Now began the greatest and most dramatic crisis of John's life. In 1577 he was kidnapped and imprisoned by his Order. Each evening he was forced to eat kneeling down and was struck with a lash. After six months a new jailer furnished him with paper and ink. In a sparsely lit cell and under harsh conditions, John wrote two of his spiritual classics, *The Dark Night* and *The Living Flame of Love*. After almost one year in prison he realized that he would not be released until he renounced the reform. One night, making a cloth rope, he let himself down from the high prison window. He was welcomed by Saint Teresa's nuns in Toledo. Eventually John was transferred to a remote monastery, La Penuela, to prepare for an assignment in Mexico. Instead he became very sick and was sent to Ubeda, where he died on December 14, 1591.

Saint John is known as Spain's greatest lyrical poet. His books, *The Ascent of Mount Carmel, The Spiritual Canticle, The Living Flame of Love*, and *The Dark Night*, are remarkable road signs for us on the mystical road to union with God. In 1926 Saint John of the Cross was declared a Doctor of the Church.

In life we pass through various phases. Transition can be difficult, especially today when we long for stability in a changing world. Practicing faith while continually readjusting to new circumstances is challenging enough, but in times of crisis or traumatic experience we can feel overwhelmed. Our former way of seeing and choosing no longer works. It is in these circumstances that the invitation to transformation is given.

One day, as I walked down the steps to the subway in New York City. I found the tunnel deserted. The light was dim. The air didn't stir. The surroundings mirrored my inner emptiness. I felt very alone. Then, from somewhere in the shadows, music from a single violin reached through my desolation. Not only is someone else here, I thought, this someone has been here before and knows this is a good place.

That violinist was like Saint John of the Cross sounding the mystery of God. God's eternal silence is sung in John's writings, so that our soul can hear it described in words that speak of desire: bride, garden, hidden fountain, darkness, healing, bridegroom, beloved. The journey through crises is a journey toward new birth. To be Christian is not to maintain, it is to transform. To reach our destination we wait, listen, and set out. Waiting implies staying in a solitary place while longing to arrive. It means moving onto the train, where we remain standing. Once the door opens, we walk out into God's loving gaze, reflected on our face.

John crossed the boundary of suffering seeking his beloved. As our companion, he lets us in on the secret way to serenity in the midst of a dark, pathless night. What we love and what we have lost reawaken us to a new encounter with the Divine. John presents the night as an inflow of God, more lovely than the dawn. Let yourself be carried by God, he encourages. God loves that you may love God with the love God has for you. This love is "poured into our hearts through the Holy Spirit" (Rom 5:5), the spring that flows and runs, although it is night.

I

Dark Night of the Soul

One dark night,
fired with love's urgent longings
—ah, the sheer grace!—
I went out unseen,
my house being now all stilled.[3]

Souls begin to enter this dark night when God, gradually drawing them out of the state of beginners (those who practice meditation on the spiritual road), begins to place them in the state of proficients (those who are already contemplatives), so that by passing through this

1

state they might reach that of the perfect, which is the divine union of the soul with God.

We should first mention here some characteristics of beginners, for the sake of a better explanation and understanding of the nature of this night and of God's motive for placing the soul in it. Although our treatment of these things will be as brief as possible, it will help beginners understand the feebleness of their state and take courage and desire that God place them in this night where the soul is strengthened in virtue and fortified for the inestimable delights of the love of God. . . .

It should be known, then, that God nurtures and caresses the soul, after it has been resolutely converted to his service, like a loving mother who warms her child with the heat of her bosom, nurses it with good milk and tender food, and carries and caresses it in her arms. But as the child grows older, the mother withholds her caresses and hides her tender love; she rubs bitter aloes on her sweet breast and sets the child down from her arms, letting it walk on its own feet so that it may put aside the habits of childhood and grow accustomed to greater and more important things. The grace of God acts just as a loving mother by re-engendering in the soul new enthusiasm and fervor in the service of God. With no effort on the soul's part, this grace causes it to taste sweet and delectable milk and to experience intense satisfaction in the performance of spiritual exercises, because God is handing the breast of his tender love to the soul, just as if it were a delicate child (1 Pet 2:2–3).

— Excerpts from: *The Dark Night*, Book 1: Chapter 1:1, 2

II

O, Guiding Night!

No matter how much individuals do through their own efforts, they cannot actively purify themselves enough to be disposed in the least degree for the divine union of the perfection of love. God must take over and purge them in that fire that is dark for them, as we will explain.

———— ❧ ————

This night . . . causes two kinds of darkness or purgation in spiritual persons according to the two parts of the soul, the sensory and the spiritual. Hence one night of purgation is sensory, by which the senses are purged and accommodated to the spirit; and the other night or purgation is spiritual, by which the spirit is purged and denuded as well as accommodated and prepared for union with God through love.

———— ᴥ ————

Since the conduct of these beginners in the way of God is lowly and not too distant from love of pleasure and of self . . . God desires to withdraw them from this base manner of loving and lead them on to a higher degree of divine love. And he desires to liberate them from the lowly exercise of the senses and of discursive meditation, by which they go in search of him so inadequately and with so many difficulties, and lead them into the exercise of spirit, in which they become capable of a communion with God that is more abundant and more free of imperfections. God does this after beginners have exercised themselves for a time in the way of virtue and have persevered in meditation and prayer. For it is through the delight and satisfaction they experience in prayer that they have become detached from worldly things and have gained some spiritual strength in God. This strength has helped them somewhat to restrain their appetites for creatures, and through it they will be able to suffer a little oppression and dryness without turning back. Consequently, it is at the time they are going about their spiritual exercises with delight and satisfaction, when in their opinion the sun of divine favor is shining most brightly on them, that God darkens all this light and closes the door and the spring of sweet spiritual water they were tasting as often and as long as they desired. For since they were weak and tender, no door was closed to them, as Saint John says in the Book of Revelation (Rev 3:8). God now leaves them in such darkness that they do not know which way to turn in their discursive imaginings. They cannot advance a step in meditation, as they used to, now that the interior sense faculties are engulfed in this night. He leaves them in such dryness that they not only fail to receive satisfaction and pleasure from their spiritual exercises and works, as they formerly did, but also find these exercises distasteful and bitter. As I said, when God sees that they have grown a little, he weans them from the sweet breast so that they might be strengthened, lays aside their swaddling bands, and puts them down from his arms that they may grow accustomed to walking by themselves. This change is a surprise to them because everything seems to be functioning in reverse.

If His Majesty intends to lead the soul on, he does not put it in this dark night of spirit immediately after its going out from the aridities and trials of the first purgation and night of sense. Instead, after having emerged from the state of beginners, the soul usually spends many years exercising itself in the state of proficients. In this new state, as one liberated from a cramped prison cell, it goes about the things of God with much more freedom and satisfaction of spirit and with more abundant interior delight than it did in the beginning before entering the night of sense. Its imagination and faculties are no longer bound to discursive meditation and spiritual solicitude, as was their custom. The soul readily finds in its spirit, without the work of meditation, a very serene, loving contemplation and spiritual delight. Nonetheless, the purgation of the soul is not complete. . . . These morsels of dark contemplation, though, are never as intense as is that frightful night of contemplation we are about to describe, in which God places the soul purposely in order to bring it to divine union.

— Excerpts from: *The Dark Night*,
Book 1: Chapters 3:3; 8:1, 3; Book 2: Chapter 1:1

III

The Way of Contemplation

Since these souls do not get satisfaction or consolation from the things of God, they do not get any from creatures either. Since God puts a soul in this dark night in order to dry up and purge its sensory appetite, he does not allow it to find sweetness or delight in anything. . . . Those suffering from the purgative dryness are ordinarily solicitous, concerned, and pained about not serving God. Even though the dryness may be furthered by melancholia or some other humor—as it often is—it does not thereby fail to produce its purgative effect in the appetite, for the soul will be deprived of every satisfaction and concerned only about God. . . . The reason for this dryness is that God transfers his goods and strength from sense to spirit. Since the sensory part of the soul is incapable of the goods of spirit, it remains deprived, dry, and empty. Thus, while the spirit is tasting, the flesh tastes nothing at all and becomes weak in its work. But through this nourishment the spirit grows stronger and more alert, and becomes more solicitous than before about not failing God.

Yet, as I say, when these aridities are the outcome of the purgative way of the sensory appetite, the spirit feels the strength and energy to work, which is obtained from the substance of that interior food, even though in the beginning it may not experience the savor, for the reason just mentioned. This food is the beginning of a contemplation that is dark and dry to the senses. Ordinarily this contemplation, which is secret and hidden from the very one who receives it, imparts to the soul, together with the dryness and emptiness it produces in the senses, an inclination to remain alone and in quietude. And the soul will be unable to dwell on any particular thought, nor will it have the desire to do so.

If those in whom this occurs know how to remain quiet, without care or solicitude about any interior or exterior work, they will soon in that unconcern and idleness delicately experience the interior nourishment. This reflection is so delicate that usually if the soul desires or tries to experience it, it cannot do so. For, as I say, this contemplation is active while the soul is in idleness and unconcern. It is like air that escapes when one tries to grasp it in one's hand.

———— ∾ ————

When spiritual persons cannot meditate, they should learn to remain in God's presence with a loving attention and a tranquil intellect . . . For little by little and very soon the divine calm and peace with a wondrous, sublime knowledge of God, enveloped in divine love, will be infused into their souls.

———— ∾ ————

. . . . At this time a person's own efforts are of no avail, but are an obstacle to the interior peace and work God is producing in the spirit through that dryness of sense. Since this peace is something spiritual and delicate, its fruit is quiet, delicate, solitary, satisfying, and peaceful, and far removed from all the other gratifications of beginners, which are very palpable and sensory.

— Excerpts from: *The Dark Night*, Book 1: Chapter 9:2, 3, 4, 6, 7
The Ascent of Mount Carmel, Book 2: Chapter 15:5

IV

Going Through

Spiritual persons suffer considerable affliction in this night, owing not so much to the aridities they undergo as to their fear of having gone astray. Since they do not find any support or satisfaction in good things, they believe there will be no more spiritual blessings for them and that God has abandoned them.

They then grow weary and strive, as was their custom, to concentrate their faculties with some satisfaction on a subject of meditation, and they think that if they do not do this and do not feel that they are at work, they are doing nothing. This effort of theirs is accompanied by an interior reluctance and repugnance on the part of the soul, for it would be pleased to dwell in that quietude and idleness without working with the faculties.

They consequently impair God's work and do not profit by their own. In searching for spirit, they lose the spirit that was the source of their tranquility and peace. They are like someone who turns from what has already been done in order to do it again, or like one who leaves a city only to reenter it, or they are like a hunter who abandons the prey in order to go hunting again. It is useless, then, for the soul to try to meditate because it will no longer profit by this exercise.

If there is no one to understand these persons, they either turn back and abandon the road or lose courage, or at least they hinder their own progress because of their excessive diligence in treading the path of discursive meditation. They fatigue and overwork themselves, thinking that they are failing because of their negligence or sins. Meditation is now useless for them because God is conducting them along another road, which is contemplation and is very different from the first, for the one road belongs to discursive meditation and the other is beyond the range of the imagination and discursive reflection.

Those who are in this situation should feel comforted; they ought to persevere patiently and not be afflicted. Let them trust in God who does not fail those who seek him with a simple and righteous heart; nor will he fail to impart what is needful for the way until getting them to the clear and pure light of love. God will give them this light by means of that other night, the night of spirit, if they merit that he place them in it. . . . All that is required of them here is freedom of soul, that they liberate themselves from the impediment and fatigue of ideas and thoughts, and care not about thinking and meditating. They must be content simply with a loving and peaceful attentiveness to God, and live without the concern, without the effort, and without the desire to taste or feel him. All these desires disquiet the soul and distract it from the peaceful, quiet, and sweet idleness of the contemplation that is being communicated to it.

And even though more scruples come to the fore concerning the loss of time and the advantages of doing something else, since it cannot do anything or think of anything in prayer, the soul should endure them peacefully, as though going to prayer means remaining in ease and freedom of spirit. If individuals were to desire to do something themselves with their interior faculties, they would hinder and lose the goods that God engraves on their souls through that peace and idleness.

If a model for the painting or retouching of a portrait should move because of a desire to do something, the artist would be unable to finish and the work would be spoiled. Similarly, any operation, affection, or thought a soul might cling to when it wants to abide in interior peace and idleness would cause distraction and disquietude, and make it feel sensory dryness and emptiness. The more a person seeks some support in knowledge and affection the more the soul will feel the lack of these, for this support cannot be supplied through these sensory means.

Accordingly, such persons should not mind if the operations of their faculties are being lost to them; they should desire rather that this be done quickly so they may be no obstacle to the operation of the infused contemplation God is bestowing, so they may receive it with more peaceful plenitude and make room in the spirit for the enkindling and burning of the love that this dark and secret contemplation bears and communicates to the soul. For contemplation is nothing else than a secret and peaceful and loving inflow of God, which, if not hampered, fires the soul in the spirit of love . . .

— Excerpts from: *The Dark Night*, Book 1:
Chapter 10:1, 2, 3, 4, 5–6

V

Living Flame of Love

The soul . . . is so inwardly transformed in the fire of love and elevated by it that it is not merely united to this fire but produces within it a living flame. . . . Since this flame is a flame of divine life, it wounds the soul with the tenderness of God's life, and it wounds and stirs it so deeply as to make it dissolve in love.

⎯⎯⎯ ⚘ ⎯⎯⎯

The soul's center is God. When it has reached God with all the capacity of its being and the strength of its operation and inclination, it will have attained its final and deepest center in God; it will know, love, and enjoy God with all its might. When it has not reached this point (as happens in this mortal life, in which the soul cannot reach God with all its strength, even though in its center—which is God through grace and his self-communication to it), it still has movement and strength for advancing further and is not satisfied. Although it is in its center, it is not yet in its deepest center, for it can go deeper in God.

This suffering resembles that of purgatory. Just as the spirits suffer purgation there so as to be able to see God through clear vision in the next life, souls in their own way suffer purgation here on earth so as to be able to be transformed in him through love in this life.

Let it suffice to know that the very God who desires to enter within the soul through the union and transformation of love is he who first assails and purges it with the light and heat of his divine flame, just as the fire that penetrates the log of wood is the same that first prepares it for this, as we said. Hence the very flame that is now gentle, since it has entered within the soul, is what was formerly oppressive, assailing it from without.

. . . [T]his highest union cannot be wrought in a soul that is not fortified by trials and temptations, and purified by tribulations, darknesses, and distress, just as a superior quality liqueur is poured only into a sturdy flask that is prepared and purified. By these trials the sensory part of the soul is purified and strengthened, and the spiritual part is refined, purged, and disposed. Since unpurified souls must undergo the sufferings of fire in the next life to attain union with God in glory, so in this life they must undergo the fire of these sufferings to reach the union of perfection. This fire acts on some more vigorously than on others, and on some for a longer time than on others, according to the degree of union to which God wishes to raise them, and according to what they must be purged of.

— Excerpts from: *The Living Flame of Love*, Prologue 4:
Stanzas 1:7, 12, 24, 25; 2:25

VI

Thirsting for the Living God

The fire of love is not commonly felt at the outset, either because it does not have a chance to take hold, owing to the impurity of the sensory part, or because the soul for want of understanding has not made within itself a peaceful place for it; although at times with or without these conditions a person will begin to feel a certain longing for God. In the measure that the fire increases, the soul becomes aware of being attracted by the love of God and enkindled in it, without knowing how or where this attraction and love originates. At times this flame and enkindling increase to such an extent that the soul desires God with urgent longings of love, as David, while in this night, said of himself: *Because my heart was inflamed* (in contemplative love), *my reins were likewise changed* (Ps 73:21). That is, my appetites of sensible affection were changed from the sensory life to the spiritual life, which implies dryness and cessation of all those appetites we are speaking of. And, he says: *I was brought to nothing and annihilated, and I knew not* (Ps 73:22). For, as we pointed out, the soul, with no knowledge of its destination, sees itself annihilated in all heavenly and earthly things in which it formerly found satisfaction; and it only sees that it is enamored, but knows not how.

Because the enkindling of love in the spirit sometimes increases exceedingly, the longings for God become so intense that it will seem to such persons that their bones are drying up in this thirst, their nature withering away, and their ardor and strength diminishing through the liveliness of the thirst of love. They will feel that this is a living thirst. David also had such experience when he proclaimed: *My soul thirsts for the living God* (Ps 43:3).

. . . [I]ndividuals generally do not perceive this love in the beginning, but they experience rather the dryness and void we are speaking of. Then, instead of this love which is enkindled afterward, they harbor, in the midst of the dryness and emptiness of their faculties, a habitual care and solicitude for God accompanied by grief or fear about not serving him. It is a sacrifice most pleasing to God—that of a spirit in distress and solicitude for his love (Ps 51:17).

Secret contemplation produces this solicitude and concern in the soul until, after having somewhat purged the sensory part of its natural propensities by means of this aridity, it begins to enkindle in the spirit this divine love. Meanwhile, however, as in one who is undergoing a cure, all is suffering in this dark and dry purgation of the appetite, and the soul being relieved of numerous imperfections acquires many virtues, thereby becoming capable of this love, as will be shown in the explanation of the following verse:—ah, the sheer grace!

— Excerpts from: *The Dark Night*, Book 1: Chapter 11:1, 2

VII

Parched and Dry

For a more complete proof of the efficacy of this sensory night in producing through its dryness and destitution the light here received from God, we will quote that passage from David in which the great power of this night in relation to the lofty knowledge of God is clearly shown. He proclaims: *In a desert land, without water, dry, and without a way, I appeared before you to be able to see your power and your glory* (Ps 63:1–2). David's teaching here is admirable: that the means to the knowledge of the glory of God were not the many spiritual delights and gratifications he had received, but the sensory aridities and detachments referred to by the dry and desert land. And it is also wonderful that, as he says, the way to the experience and vision of the power of God did not consist in ideas and meditations about God, of which he had made extensive use. But it consisted in not being able either to grasp God with ideas or walk by means of discursive, imaginative meditation, which is here indicated by the land without a way. . . .

In the dryness and emptiness of this night of the appetite, a person also procures spiritual humility, that virtue opposed to the first capital vice, spiritual pride. Through this humility acquired by means of self-knowledge, individuals are purged of all those imperfections of the vice of pride into which they fell in the time of their prosperity.

From this humility stems love of neighbor, for they esteem them and do not judge them as they did before when they were aware that they enjoyed an intense fervor while others did not.

These persons know only their own misery and keep it so much in sight that they have no opportunity to watch anyone else's conduct. David while in this night gives an admirable manifestation of such a state of soul: *I became dumb, and was humbled, and I kept silent in good things, and my sorrow was renewed* (Ps 39:2). He says this because it seemed to him that his blessings had so come to an end that not only was he unable to find words for them, but he also became silent concerning his neighbor, in the sorrow he experienced from the knowledge of his own misery.

These individuals also become submissive and obedient in their spiritual journey. Since they are so aware of their own wretchedness, they not only listen to the teaching of others but even desire to be directed and told what to do by anyone at all. The affective presumption they sometimes had in their prosperity leaves them. And, finally, as they proceed on their journey, all the other imperfections of this first vice, spiritual pride, are swept away.

—Excerpts from: *The Dark Night*, Book 1: Chapter 12:6, 7, 8

VIII

Benefits of the Dark Night

God so curbs concupiscence and bridles the appetite through this arid and dark night that the soul cannot feast on any sensory delight from earthly or heavenly things, and he continues this purgation in such a way that the concupiscence and the appetites are brought into subjection, reformed, and mortified. The passions, as a result, lose their strength and become sterile from not receiving any satisfaction, just as the courses of the udder dry up when milk is not drawn through them daily.

Once the soul's appetites have withered, and it lives in spiritual sobriety, admirable benefits besides those mentioned result. For when the appetites and concupiscences are quenched, the soul dwells in spiritual peace and tranquility.

. . . [T]he soul bears a habitual remembrance of God, accompanied by a fear and dread of turning back on the spiritual road. . . . Another very great benefit for the soul in this night is that it exercises all the virtues together. In the patience and forbearance practiced in these voids and aridities, and through perseverance in its spiritual exercises without consolation or satisfaction, the soul practices the love of God. . . .

David affirms that a person obtains in this night these four benefits: the delight of peace; a habitual remembrance of God and solicitude concerning him; cleanness and purity of soul; and the practice of virtue. For David himself had such experience by being in this night: *My soul refused consolations, I remembered God and found consolation, and exercised myself, and my soul swooned away*; and then he adds: *I meditated at night in my heart, and I exercised myself, and swept and purified my spirit* (of all its imperfections) (Ps 77:2–6).

Finally, insofar as these persons are purged of their sensory affections and appetites, they obtain freedom of spirit in which they acquire the twelve fruits of the Holy Spirit.

They are also wondrously liberated from the hands of their enemies, the devil, the world, and the flesh. For when the sensory delight and gratification regarding things is quenched, neither the devil, nor the world, nor sensuality has arms or power against the spirit.

— Excerpts from: *The Dark Night*, Book 1:
Chapter 13:3, 4, 5, 6, 11

IX

From the Hands of God

People, then, should live with great patience and constancy in all the tribulations and trials God places on them, whether they be exterior or interior, spiritual or bodily, great or small, and they should accept them all as from God's hand as a good remedy and not flee from them, for they bring health. In this matter let them take the counsel of the Wise Man: *If the spirit of he who has power descends upon you, do not abandon your place* (the place and site of your probation, which is the trial he sends you), *for the cure will make great sins cease* (Eccles 10:4); that is, it will cut off the roots of your sins and imperfections—your evil habits. The combat of trials, distress, and temptations deadens the evil and imperfect habits of the soul and purifies and strengthens it. People should hold in esteem the interior and exterior trials God sends them, realizing that there are few who merit to be brought to perfection through suffering and to undergo trials for the sake of so high a state.

In this matter it is worth noting the difference between the possession of God through grace in itself and the possession of him through union, for one lies in loving and the other lies also in communicating. The difference resembles that between betrothal and marriage.

In betrothal there is only a mutual agreement and willingness between the two, and the bridegroom graciously gives jewels and ornaments to his betrothed. But in marriage there is also a communication and union between the persons. Although the bridegroom sometimes visits the bride in the betrothal and brings her presents, as we said, there is no union of persons, nor does this fall within the scope of betrothal.

Likewise, when the soul has reached such purity in itself and its faculties that the will is very pure and purged of other alien satisfactions and appetites in the inferior and superior parts, and has rendered its "yes" to God concerning all of this, since now God's will and the soul's are one through their own free consent, then the soul has attained possession of God insofar as this is possible by way of the will and grace. And this means that in the "yes" of the soul, God has given the true and complete "yes" of his grace.

— Excerpts from: *The Living Flame of Love*, Stanzas 2:30; 3:24

X

My House Being Now All Stilled

This dark night is an inflow of God into the soul, which purges it of its habitual ignorances and imperfections, natural and spiritual, and which the contemplatives call infused contemplation or mystical theology. Through this contemplation, God teaches the soul secretly and instructs it in the perfection of love without its doing anything or understanding how this happens.

Insofar as infused contemplation is loving wisdom of God, it produces two principal effects in the soul: by both purging and illumining, this contemplation prepares the soul for union with God through love. Hence the same loving wisdom that purges and illumines the blessed spirits purges and illumines the soul here on earth.

The soul had to go out to accomplish so heroic and rare a feat—to be united with its divine Beloved outside—because the Beloved is not found except alone, outside, and in solitude. . . . It must go out at night when all the members of its house are asleep, that is, when the lower operations, passions, and appetites of its soul are put to sleep or quelled by means of this night . . . All natural ability is insufficient to produce the supernatural goods that God alone infuses in the soul passively, secretly, and in silence.

The soul then states that "fired with love's urgent longings" it passed through this dark night of the sense to union with the Beloved. . . . To achieve this liberation it was advantageous for the soul to depart in the dark night, that is, in the privation of all satisfactions and in the mortification of all the appetites. . . . "My house being now all stilled."

It was a sheer grace for this soul that God in this night puts to sleep all the members of its household, that is, all the faculties, passions, affections, and appetites that live in its sensory and spiritual parts. God puts them to sleep to enable the soul to go out to the spiritual union of the perfect love of God without being seen, that is, without the hindrance of these affections. . . .

In this night the soul subtly escapes from its enemies, who were always opposed to its departure. In its journey in the darkness of this night . . . it departs by a very secret ladder of which no one in the house knows. This ladder, as we will also explain, is the living faith by which it departs in so concealed a way in order to carry out its plan successfully, and by which it cannot but escape very securely. The soul is particularly secure in this purgative night because its appetites, affections, passions, and so on, were put to sleep, mortified, and deadened. These are the members of the household that when awake and alive would not consent to this departure.

— Excerpts from: *The Dark Night*, Book 2: Chapters 5:1; 14:1, 2; 15:1
The Ascent of Mount Carmel, Book 1: Chapters 14:2; 15:2

XI

A Ray of Darkness

When this purgative contemplation oppresses a soul, it feels very vividly indeed the shadow of death, the sighs of death, and the sorrows of hell, all of which reflect the feeling of God's absence, of being chastised and rejected by him, and of being unworthy of him, as well as the object of his anger. The soul experiences all this and even more, for now it seems that this affliction will last forever.

Such persons also feel forsaken and despised by creatures, particularly by their friends. David immediately adds: *You have withdrawn my friends and acquaintances far from me; they have considered me an abomination* (Ps 88:8). Jonah, as one who also underwent this experience, both physically and spiritually in the belly of the whale, testifies: *You have cast me out into the deep, into the heart of the sea, and the current surrounded me; all its whirlpools and waves passed over me and I said: I am cast from the sight of your eyes; yet I shall see your holy temple again* (he says this because God purifies the soul that it might see his temple); *the waters encircled me even to the soul, the abyss went round about me, the open sea covered my head, I descended to the lowest parts of the mountains, the locks of the earth closed me up forever* (Jon 2:4–7). The "locks" refer to the soul's imperfections that hinder it from enjoying the delights of this contemplation.

God does all this by means of dark contemplation. And the soul not only suffers the void and suspension of these natural supports and apprehensions, which is a terrible anguish (like hanging in midair, unable to breathe), but it is also purged by this contemplation. As fire consumes the tarnish and rust of metal, this contemplation annihilates, empties, and consumes all the affections and imperfect habits the soul contracted throughout its life. Since these imperfections are deeply rooted in the substance of the soul, in addition to this poverty, this natural and spiritual emptiness, it usually suffers an oppressive undoing and an inner torment. Thus the passage of Ezekiel may be verified: *Heap together the bones, and I shall burn them in the fire, the flesh shall be consumed, and the whole composition burned, and the bones destroyed* (Ezek 24:10). He refers here to the affliction suffered in the emptiness and poverty of both the sensory and the spiritual substance of the soul. And he then adds: *Place it also thus empty on the embers that its metal may become hot and melt and its uncleanness be taken away from it and its rust consumed* (Ezek 24:11). This passage points out the heavy affliction the soul suffers from the purgation caused by the fire of this contemplation. For the prophet asserts that in order to burn away the rust of the affections the soul must, as it were, be annihilated and undone in the measure that these passions and imperfections are connatural to it.

Because the soul is purified in this forge *like gold in the crucible*, as the Wise Man says (Wis 3:6), it feels both this terrible undoing in its very substance and extreme poverty as though it were approaching its end. This experience is expressed in David's cry: *Save me, Lord, for the waters have come in even unto my soul; I am stuck in the mire of the deep, and there is nowhere to stand; I have come unto the depth of the sea, and the tempest has overwhelmed me. I have labored in crying out, my throat has become hoarse, my eyes have failed while I hope in my God* (Ps 69:1–3).

God humbles the soul greatly in order to exalt it greatly afterward. And if he did not ordain that these feelings, when quickened in the soul, be soon put to sleep again, a person would die in a few days. Only at intervals is one aware of these feelings in all their intensity. Sometimes this experience is so vivid that it seems to the soul that it sees hell and perdition open before it. These are the ones who go down into hell alive (Ps 55:15), since their purgation on earth is similar to what takes place there. For this purgation is what would have to be undergone there. The soul that endures it here on earth either does not enter that place, or is detained there for only a short while. It gains more in one hour here on earth by this purgation than it would in many there.

— Excerpts from: *The Dark Night*, Book 2: Chapter 6:2, 3, 5–6

XII

Duration of the Dark Night

B ut if it is to be truly efficacious, it will last for some years, no matter how intense it may be; although there are intervals in which, through God's dispensation, this dark contemplation ceases to assail the soul in a purgative mode and shines upon it illuminatively and lovingly. Then the soul, like one who has been unshackled and released from a dungeon and who can enjoy the benefit of spaciousness and freedom, experiences great sweetness of peace and loving friendship with God in a ready abundance of spiritual communication.

Thus, although persons suffering this purgation know that they love God and that they would give a thousand lives for him (they would indeed, for souls undergoing these trials love God very earnestly), they find no relief. This knowledge instead causes them deeper affliction. For in loving God so intensely that nothing else gives them concern, and aware of their own misery, they are unable to believe that God loves them. They believe that they neither have nor ever will have within themselves anything deserving of God's love, but rather every reason for being abhorred not only by God but by every creature forever. They grieve to see within themselves reasons for meriting rejection by him whom they so love and long for.

It seems incredible that the brighter and purer the supernatural, divine light is, the darker it is for the soul; and that the less bright it is, the less dark it is to the soul. We can understand this truth clearly if we consider what we proved above from the teaching of the Philosopher[4]: that the clearer and more evident supernatural things are in themselves, the darker they are to our intellects.

This is precisely what the divine ray of contemplation does. In striking the soul with its divine light, it surpasses the natural light and thereby darkens and deprives a soul of all the natural affections and apprehensions it perceived by means of its natural light. It leaves a person's spiritual and natural faculties not only in darkness, but in emptiness too. Leaving the soul thus empty and dark, the ray purges and illumines it with divine spiritual light. . . .

And this is characteristic of the spirit purged and annihilated of all particular knowledge and affection: Not finding satisfaction in anything or understanding anything in particular, and remaining in its emptiness and darkness, it embraces all things with great preparedness. And Saint Paul's words are verified: *Nihil habentes, et omnia possidentes* "Having nothing, yet possessing all things" (2 Cor 6:10). Such poverty of spirit deserves this blessedness.

It remains to be said, then, that even though this happy night darkens the spirit, it does so only to impart light concerning all things; and even though it humbles individuals and reveals their miseries, it does so only to exalt them; and even though it impoverishes and empties them of all possessions and natural affection, it does so only that they may reach out divinely to the enjoyment of all earthly and heavenly things, with a general freedom of spirit in them all.

———— ∽ ————

Furthermore, in this union for which the dark night is a preparation, the soul in its communion with God must be endowed and filled with a certain glorious splendor embodying innumerable delights. These delights surpass all the abundance the soul can possess naturally, for nature, so weak and impure, cannot receive these delights, as Isaiah says: *Eye has not seen, nor ear heard, nor has it entered any human heart what he has prepared* (Is 64:4). As a result the soul must first be set in emptiness and poverty of spirit and purged of every natural support, consolation, and apprehension, earthly and heavenly. Thus empty, it is truly poor in spirit and stripped of the old self, and thereby able to live that new and blessed life which is the state of union with God, attained by means of this night.

— Excerpts from: *The Dark Night*, Book 2:
Chapters 7:4, 7; 8:2, 4, 5; 9:1, 4

XIII

God Seeks the Beloved

In the first place it should be known that if anyone is seeking God, the Beloved is seeking that person much more.

. . . God does not fit in an occupied heart. In this matter of striving for perfection, not to turn back is to go forward; and the intellect goes forward by establishing itself more in faith. Thus it advances by darkening itself, for faith is darkness to the intellect. Since the intellect cannot understand the nature of God, it must journey in surrender to him rather than by understanding, and thus it advances by not understanding.

"Or," you will say, "when the intellect does not understand particular things, the will is idle and does not love (something that must always be avoided on the spiritual road), because the will can only love what the intellect understands." This is true, especially in the natural operations and acts of the soul in which the will does not love except what the intellect understands distinctly. But in the contemplation we are discussing (by which God infuses himself into the soul), particular knowledge as well as acts made by the soul are unnecessary. The reason for this is that God in one act is communicating light and love together, which is loving supernatural knowledge. We can assert that this knowledge is like light that transmits heat, for that light also enkindles love. This knowledge is general and dark to the intellect because it is contemplative knowledge, which is a ray of darkness for the intellect, as Saint Dionysius teaches.

Love is therefore present in the will in the manner that knowledge is present in the intellect. Just as this knowledge infused by God in the intellect is general and dark, devoid of particular understanding, the love in the will is also general, without any clarity arising from particular understanding. Since God is divine light and love in his communication of himself to the soul, he equally informs these two faculties (intellect and will) with knowledge and love. Since God is unintelligible in this life, knowledge of him is dark, as I say, and the love present in the will is fashioned after this knowledge. Yet sometimes in this delicate communication God wounds and communicates himself to one faculty more than to the other; sometimes more knowledge is experienced than love, and at other times more love than knowledge; and likewise at times all knowledge is felt without any love, or all love without any knowledge.

To journey to God, the will must walk in detachment from every pleasant thing, rather than in attachment to it. It thus carries out well the commandment of love, which is to love God above all things; this cannot be done without nakedness and emptiness concerning them all.

— Excerpts from: *The Living Flame of Love*, Stanzas 3:28, 48–49, 51

XIV

Wood Transformed in the Fire

For the sake of further clarity in this matter, we ought to note that this purgative and loving knowledge, or divine light we are speaking of, has the same effect on a soul that fire has on a log of wood. The soul is purged and prepared for union with the divine light just as the wood is prepared for transformation into the fire. Fire, when applied to wood, first dehumidifies it, dispelling all moisture and making it give off any water it contains. Then it gradually turns the wood black, makes it dark and ugly, and even causes it to emit a bad odor. By drying out the wood, the fire brings to light and expels all those ugly and dark accidents that are contrary to fire. Finally, by heating and enkindling it from without, the fire transforms the wood into itself and makes it as beautiful as it is itself. Once transformed, the wood no longer has any activity or passivity of its own, except for its weight and its quantity that is denser than the fire. It possesses the properties and performs the actions of fire: It is dry and it dries; it is hot and it gives off heat; it is brilliant and it illumines; it is also much lighter in weight than before. It is the fire that produces all these properties in the wood.

Similarly, we should philosophize about this divine, loving fire of contemplation. Before transforming the soul, it purges it of all contrary qualities. It produces blackness and darkness and brings to the fore the soul's ugliness; thus one seems worse than before and unsightly and abominable. This divine purge stirs up all the foul and vicious humors of which the soul was never before aware; never did it realize there was so much evil in itself, since these humors were so deeply rooted. And now that they may be expelled and annihilated they are brought to light and seen clearly through the illumination of this dark light of divine contemplation.

<hr>

. . . [W]e deduce that as the soul is purged and purified by this fire of love, it is further enkindled in love, just as the wood becomes hotter as the fire prepares it. Individuals, however, do not always feel this enkindling of love. But sometimes the contemplation shines less forcibly so they may have the opportunity to observe and even rejoice over the work being achieved, for then these good effects are revealed. It is as though one were to stop work and take the iron out of the forge to observe what is being accomplished. Thus the soul is able to perceive the good it was unaware of while the work was proceeding. So too, when the flame stops acting upon the wood, there is a chance to see how much the wood has been enkindled by it.

— Excerpts from: *The Dark Night*, Book 2:
Chapter 10:1–2, 6

XV

Love's Urgent Longings

The touch of this divine love and fire so dries up the spirit and so enkindles the soul's longings to slake its thirst for this love that such persons go over these longings in their mind a thousand times and pine for God in a thousand ways. David expresses this state very well in a psalm: *My soul thirsts for you; in how many ways does my flesh long for you* (Ps 63:1), that is, in its desires. And another translation puts it this way: *My soul thirsts for you, my soul loses itself or dies for you.*

As a result the soul proclaims in this verse: "with love's urgent longings," and not, "with an urgent longing of love." In all its thoughts and in all its business and in all events, it loves in many ways, and desires, and also suffers in its desire in many ways, and at all times and in many places. It finds rest in nothing, for it feels this anxiety in the burning wound, as the prophet Job explains: *As the servant desires the shade and as the hireling desires the end of his work, so have I had empty months and numbered to myself long and wearisome nights. If I lie down to sleep I shall say: When will I arise? And then I will await the evening and will be filled with sorrows until the darkness of the night* (Job 7:2–4).

❦

Nonetheless, in the midst of these dark and loving afflictions, the soul feels a certain companionship and an interior strength; these so fortify and accompany it that when this weight of anxious darkness passes, the soul often feels alone, empty, and weak. The reason is that since the strength and efficacy of the dark fire of love that assails it is communicated and impressed on it passively, the darkness, strength, and warmth of love cease when the assault terminates.

❦

The soul does not always feel this inflaming and anxious longing of love. In the beginning of the spiritual purgation, the divine fire spends itself in drying out and preparing the wood—that is, the soul—rather than in heating it. Yet as time passes and the fire begins to give off heat, the soul usually experiences the burning and warmth of love.

As the intellect becomes more purged by means of this darkness, it happens sometimes that this mystical and loving theology, besides inflaming the will, also wounds the intellect by illumining it with some knowledge and light so delightfully and delicately that the will is thereby marvelously enkindled in fervor. This divine fire burns in the will—while the will remains passive—like a living flame and in such a way that this love now seems to be a live fire because of the living knowledge communicated.

— Excerpts from: *The Dark Night*, Book 2:
Chapters 11:5, 6, 7; 12:5

XVI

Mysteries of the Hidden God

It should be known that the Word, the Son of God, together with the Father and the Holy Spirit, is hidden by his essence and his presence in the innermost being of the soul. Individuals who want to find him should leave all things through affection and will, enter within themselves in deepest recollection, and let all things be as though not. Saint Augustine, addressing God in the *Soliloquies*, said: *I did not find you without, Lord, because I wrongly sought you without, who were within.* God, then, is hidden in the soul, and there the good contemplative must seek him with love, exclaiming: "Where have you hidden?"

It brings special happiness to a person to understand that God is never absent, not even from a soul in mortal sin (and how much less from one in the state of grace).

What more do you want, O soul! And what else do you search for outside, when within yourself you possess your riches, delights, satisfaction, fullness, and kingdom—your Beloved whom you desire and seek? Be joyful and gladdened in your interior recollection with him, for you have him so close to you. Desire him there, adore him there. Do not go in pursuit of him outside yourself. You will only become distracted and wearied thereby, and you shall not find him, or enjoy him more securely, or sooner, or more intimately than by seeking him within you. There is but one difficulty: Even though he does abide within you, he is hidden. Nevertheless, it is vital for you to know his hiding place so you may search for him there with assuredness. And this, soul, is also what you ask, when with the affection of love you question: "Where have you hidden?"

———— ᘓ ————

Come, then, O beautiful soul! Since you know now that your desired Beloved lives hidden within your heart, strive to be really hidden with him, and you will embrace him within you and experience him with loving affection. Note that through Isaiah he calls you to this hiding place: *Come, enter into your inner rooms, shut the door behind you* (your faculties to all creatures), *hide yourself a little, even for a moment* (Is 26:20), for this moment of life on earth. If, O soul, in this short space of time you keep diligent watch over your heart, as the Wise Man advises (Prov 4:23), God will undoubtedly give you what he also promises further on through Isaiah: *I will give you hidden treasures and reveal to you the substance and mysteries of the secrets* (Is 45:3). . . .

A ray of sunshine shining upon a smudgy window is unable to illumine that window completely and transform it into its own light. It could do this if the window were cleaned and polished. The less the film and stain are wiped away, the less the window will be illumined: and the clearer the window is, the brighter will be its illumination. The extent of illumination is not dependent upon the ray of sunlight but upon the window. If the window is totally clean and pure, the sunlight will so transform and illumine it that to all appearances the window will be identical with the ray of sunlight and shine just as the sun's ray. . . . The soul upon which the divine light of God's being is ever shining, or better, in which it is always dwelling by nature, is like this window . . .

—Excerpts from: *The Spiritual Canticle*, Stanzas 1:6, 8, 10
The Ascent of Mount Carmel, Book 2: Chapter 5:6

XVII

Wound of Love

It should be known that besides the many other different kinds of visits God grants to the soul, in which he wounds and raises it up in love, he usually bestows some secret touches of love that pierce and wound it like fiery arrows, leaving it wholly cauterized by the fire of love. And these wounds, mentioned here, are properly called wounds of love. They so inflame the will in its affection that it burns up in this flame and fire of love. So intense is this burning that the soul is seemingly consumed in that flame, and the fire makes it go out of itself, wholly renews it, and changes its manner of being, as in the case of the phoenix that burns itself in the fire and rises anew from the ashes.

⎯⎯⎯∾⎯⎯⎯

Those who seek God and yet want their own satisfaction and rest seek him at night and thus will not find him. Those who look for him through the practice and works of the virtues and get up from the bed of their own satisfaction and delight seek him by day and thus will find him.

It is noteworthy that any soul with authentic love cannot be satisfied until it really possesses God. Everything else not only fails to satisfy it but, as we said, increases the hunger and appetite to see him as he is. Every glimpse of the Beloved received through knowledge or feeling or any other communication (which is like a messenger bringing the soul news of who he is) further increases and awakens her appetite, like the crumbs given to someone who is famished. Finding it difficult to be delayed by so little, she pleads: "Now wholly surrender yourself!"

. . . My Lord, my Spouse, you have given yourself to me partially; now may you give yourself completely. You have revealed yourself to me as through fissures in a rock; now may you give me that revelation more clearly. You have communicated by means of others, as if joking with me; now may you do so truly, communicating yourself by yourself. In your visits, at times, it seems you are about to give me the jewel of possessing you; but when I become aware of this I find myself without possessing it, for you hide this jewel as if you had been joking. Now wholly surrender yourself by giving yourself entirely to all of me, so my entire soul may have complete possession of you.

— Excerpts from: *The Spiritual Canticle*, Stanzas 1:17; 3:3; 6:4, 6

XVIII

Love Alone

Mary Magdalene, in spite of her past, paid no heed to the crowds of people, prominent as well as unknown, at the banquet. She did not consider the propriety of weeping and shedding tears in the presence of our Lord's guests. Her only concern was to reach him for whom her soul was already wounded and on fire, without any delay and without waiting for another more appropriate time (Lk 7:37–38). And such is the inebriation and courage of love: Knowing that her Beloved was shut up in the tomb by a huge sealed rock and surrounded by guards so the disciples could not steal his body, she did not permit this to keep her from going out with ointments before daybreak to anoint him (Mt 27:64–66; Mk 16:1–2; Jn 20:1).

The strength and vehemence of love has this trait: Everything seems possible to it, and it believes everyone is occupied as it is; it does not believe anyone could be employed in any other way or seek anyone other than he who it seeks and loves; it believes there is nothing else to desire or to occupy it and that everyone is engaged in seeking and loving him. When the bride went searching for her Beloved in the plazas and suburbs, she thought that others were doing the same and told them that if they found him they should tell him she was suffering for love of him (Song 3:2; 5:8). Mary's love was so ardent that she thought she would go and take Jesus away, however great the impediments, if the gardener would tell where he was hidden.

Such are the traits of these longings of love that the soul experiences when it is advanced in this spiritual purgation. The wounded soul rises up at night, in this purgative darkness, according to the affections of the will; as the lioness or she-bear that goes in search of her cubs when they are taken away and cannot be found (2 Sam 17:8; Hos 13:8), it anxiously and forcibly goes out in search of its God. Since it is immersed in darkness, it feels his absence and feels that it is dying with love of him. Such is impatient love, which one cannot long endure without either receiving its object or dying . . .

It should be explained here why, even though the soul feels as miserable and unworthy of God as it does in these purgative darknesses, it possesses an energy bold enough to go out to be joined with God. . . . Once all these darknesses and imperfections are expelled, it seems that the immense benefits and goods the soul is acquiring in this happy night of contemplation begin to appear.

— Excerpts from: *The Dark Night*, Book 2: Chapter 13:6, 7, 8, 9, 10

XIX

How Love Endures

A stag wounded by a poison arrow neither rests nor remains calm, but searches everywhere for remedies, plunging now into these waters, now into those, and the effect of the poison arrow ever increases in all circumstances and with all remedies taken until finally it seizes upon the heart and the stag dies. Similarly, the soul touched by the poison arrow of love, as is this soul we are discussing, never stops seeking remedies for her sorrow. Yet she not only fails to find them, but everything she thinks, says, and does brings her greater sorrow. Conscious of this, and knowing she has no other remedy than to put herself in the hands of the one who wounded her, so that in relieving her he may slay her now entirely with the force of love. . . . Accordingly, the soul can know clearly whether or not she loves God purely. If she loves him her heart or love will not be set on herself or her own satisfaction and gain, but on pleasing God and giving him honor and glory.

Whether the heart has been truly stolen by God will be evident in either of these two signs: if it has longings for God or if it finds no satisfaction in anything but him, as the soul demonstrates here. The reason is that the heart cannot have peace and rest while not possessing, and when it is truly attracted it no longer has possession of self or of any other thing. And if it does not possess completely what it loves, it cannot help being weary, in proportion to its loss, until it possesses the loved object and is satisfied. Until this possession the soul is like an empty vessel waiting to be filled, or a hungry person craving for food, or someone sick moaning for health, or like one suspended in the air with nothing to lean on. Such is the truly loving heart.

. . . [T]he soul feels that she is rushing toward God as rapidly as a falling stone when nearing its center. She also feels that she is like wax in which an impression, though being made, is not yet complete. She knows, too, that she is like a sketch or the first draft of a drawing and calls out to the one who did this sketch to finish the painting and image. And her faith is so enlightened that it gives her a glimpse of some clear divine reflections of the height of her God. As a result she does not know what to do other than turn to this very faith that contains and hides the image and the beauty of her Beloved and from which she also receives these sketches and tokens of love . . .

———— ∾ ————

This is the meaning of Saint Paul's affirmation: *Vivo autem, iam non ego; vivit vero in me Christus,* "I live, now not I, but Christ lives in me" (Gal 2:20). In saying "I live, now not I," he meant that even though he had life it was not his because he was transformed in Christ, and it was divine more than human. He consequently asserts that he does not live but Christ lives in him. In accord with this likeness and transformation, we can say that his life and Christ's were one life through union of love. This transformation into divine life will be effected perfectly in heaven in all those who merit the vision of God. Transformed in God, these blessed souls will live the life of God and not their own life—although, indeed, it will be their own life because God's life will be theirs. Then they will truly proclaim: We live, now not we, but God lives in us.

Although transformation in this life can be what it was in Saint Paul, it still cannot be perfect and complete even though the soul reaches such transformation of love as is found in the spiritual marriage, the highest state attainable in this life. Everything can be called a sketch of love in comparison with that perfect image, the transformation in glory. Yet the attainment of such a sketch of transformation in this life is a great blessing, for with this transformation the Beloved is very pleased. Desiring the bride to put him as a sketch in her soul, he said in the Song of Songs: *Put me as a seal upon your heart, as a seal upon your arm* (Song 8:6).

In that nocturnal tranquility and silence and in knowledge of the divine light the soul becomes aware of Wisdom's wonderful harmony and sequence in the variety of her creatures and works. . . . She calls this music "silent" because it is tranquil and quiet knowledge, without the sound of voices. And thus there is in it the sweetness of music and the quietude of silence. Accordingly, she says that her Beloved is silent music because in him she knows and enjoys this symphony of spiritual music. Not only is he silent music, but he is also Sounding solitude.

— Excerpts from: *The Spiritual Canticle*,
Stanzas 9:1, 5, 6; 12:1, 8; 14:25

XX

Ah, Sheer Grace!

A person would never have been able to accomplish
this work alone . . . Accordingly, God makes the soul
die to all that he is not, so that when it is stripped and flayed
of its old skin, he may clothe it anew. Its youth is renewed
like the eagle's (Ps 103:5), clothed in the new self, which is
created, as the Apostle says, according to God (Eph 4:24).
This renovation illumines the human intellect with supernatural light so it becomes divine, united with the divine;
informs the will with love of God so it is no longer less
than divine and loves in no other way than divinely, united
and made one with the divine will and love; and is also a
divine conversion and changing of the memory, the

affections, and the appetites according to God. And thus this soul will be a soul of heaven, heavenly and more divine than human.

As we have gradually seen, God accomplishes all this work in the soul by illumining it and firing it divinely with urgent longings for God alone.

A question immediately arises here: Since the things of God in themselves produce good in the soul, are beneficial, and give assurance, why does God in this night darken the appetites and faculties so that these derive no satisfaction in such good things and find it difficult to be occupied with them—in some ways even more difficult than to be occupied with other things? The answer is that at this time there should be no activity or satisfaction relative to spiritual objects, because the soul's faculties and appetites are impure, lowly, and very natural. And even were God to give these faculties the activity and delight of supernatural, divine things, they would be unable to receive them except in their own way, very basely and naturally. As the Philosopher[5] says, *Whatever is received is received according to the mode of the receiver*.

Since these natural faculties do not have the purity, strength, or capacity to receive and taste supernatural things in a supernatural or divine mode, but only according to their own mode, which is human and lowly, as we said, these faculties must also be darkened regarding the divine, so that weaned, purged, and annihilated in their natural way they might lose that lowly and human mode of receiving and working. Thus all these faculties and appetites of the soul are tempered and prepared for the sublime reception, experience, and savor of the divine and supernatural, which cannot be received until the old self dies.

Oh, then, spiritual soul, when you see your appetites darkened, your inclinations dry and constrained, your faculties incapacitated for any interior exercise, do not be afflicted; think of this as a grace, since God is freeing you from yourself and taking from you your own activity. However well your actions may have succeeded, you did not work so completely, perfectly, and securely—because of their impurity and awkwardness—as you do now that God takes you by the hand and guides you in darkness, as though you were blind, along a way and to a place you know not. You would never have succeeded in reaching this place no matter how good your eyes and your feet.

. . . God gives grace for grace (Jn 1:16), because when God beholds the soul made attractive through grace, he is impelled to grant her more grace, for he dwells within her well pleased with her. . . . Because this grace exalts, honors, and beautifies her in his sight, God loves her ineffably. If prior to her being in grace, he loved her only on account of himself, now that she is in grace he loves her not only on account of himself but also on account of herself. And thus enamored by means of the effects and works of grace, or without them, he ever continues to communicate more love and more graces. And as he continues to honor and exalt her, he becomes continually more captivated by and enamored of her.

— Excerpts from: *The Dark Night*, Book 2: Chapters 13:11; 16:4, 7
The Spiritual Canticle, Stanza 33:7

XXI

Clothed in Beauty

Spiritual marriage is incomparably greater than the spiritual betrothal, for it is a total transformation in the Beloved, in which each surrenders the entire possession of self to the other with a certain consummation of the union of love. The soul thereby becomes divine, God through participation, insofar as is possible in this life. And thus I think that this state never occurs without the soul's being confirmed in grace, for the faith of both is confirmed when God's faith in the soul is here confirmed. It is accordingly the highest state attainable in this life.

Just as in the consummation of carnal marriage there are two in one flesh, as Sacred Scripture points out (Gen

2:24), so also when the spiritual marriage between God and the soul is consummated, there are two natures in one spirit and love, as Saint Paul says in making this same comparison: *Whoever is joined to the Lord becomes one spirit with him* (1 Cor 6:17). This union resembles the union of the light of a star or candle with the light of the sun, for what then sheds light is not the star or candle, but the sun, which has absorbed the other lights into its own.

The Bridegroom speaks of the state of union in this verse, saying, "the bride has entered," that is, she has entered, leaving behind everything temporal and natural and all spiritual affections, modes, and manners, and has set aside and forgotten all temptations, disturbances, pains, solicitude, and cares, and is transformed in this high embrace. . . .

She has been transformed into her God, here referred to as "the sweet garden," because of the sweet and pleasant dwelling she finds in him.

One does not reach this garden of full transformation, which is the joy, delight, and glory of spiritual marriage, without first passing through the spiritual betrothal and the loyal and mutual love of betrothed persons. For after the soul has been for some time the betrothed of the Son of God in gentle and complete love, God calls her and places her in his flowering garden to consummate this most joyful state of marriage with him. The union wrought between the two natures and the communication of the divine to the human in this state is such that even though neither changes its being, both appear to be God. Yet in this life the union cannot be perfect, although it is beyond words and thought.

— Excerpts from: *The Spiritual Canticle*, Stanzas 22:3-4

XXII

The Inner Wine Cellar

New lovers are comparable to new wine. They are the beginners in the service of God. The fervors of the wine of love are very exterior, in the sensory part of the soul. The lees [sediments] of the weak and imperfect sensory part have not yet finished their work of fermentation. These new lovers find their strength in the savor of love, and this sensible savor is what really motivates and strengthens them for the performance of their works. One should not trust this love until these fervors and coarse sensory tastes have passed. Just as this fervor and the warmth of sense can incline one to good and perfect love and serve as a beneficial means for such love by a thorough fermentation of the lees of imperfection, so too it is very easy in these beginnings and in this novelty of tastes for the new wine of love to fail and lose its fervor and delight.

. . . This wine cellar is the last and most intimate degree of love in which the soul can be placed in this life. . . . I drank of my Beloved. As the drink is diffused through all the members and veins of the body, so this communication is diffused substantially in the whole soul, or better, the soul is transformed in God. . . . In that sweet drink of God, in which the soul is imbibed in him, she most willingly and with intense delight surrenders herself wholly to him in the desire to be totally his and never to possess in herself anything other than him. God causes in this union the purity and perfection necessary for such surrender. And since he transforms her in himself, he makes her entirely his own and empties her of all she possesses other than him.

Hence, not only in her will but also in her works she is really and totally given to God without keeping anything back, just as God has freely given himself entirely to her. This union is so effected that the two wills are mutually paid, surrendered, and satisfied (so that neither fails the other in anything) with the fidelity and stability of an espousal.

Before reaching this gift and surrender of herself and her energy to the Beloved, the soul usually has many unprofitable occupations by which she endeavors to serve her own appetite and that of others. For we can say she had as much work as she had many habitual imperfections. These habitual imperfections can be, for example, the trait or "work" of speaking about useless things, thinking about them, and also carrying them out, not making use of such actions in accord with the demands of perfection. She usually has desires to serve the appetites of others, which she does through ostentation, compliments, flattery, human respect, the effort to impress and please people by her actions, and many other useless things. In this fashion she strives to please people, employing for them all her care, desires, work, and finally energy.

. . . [N]ow all this work is directed to the practice of love of God, that is: All the ability of my soul and body (memory, intellect, and will, interior and exterior senses, appetites of the sensory and spiritual parts) move in love and because of love. Everything I do I do with love, and everything I suffer I suffer with the delight of love.

— Excerpts from: *The Spiritual Canticle*,
Stanzas 25:10; 26:3–5; 27:6; 28:7, 8

XXIII

High Caverns on the Rock

With God, to love the soul is to put her somehow in himself and make her his equal. Thus he loves the soul within himself, with himself, that is, with the very love by which he loves himself. This is why the soul merits the love of God in all her works insofar as she does them in God.

One of the main reasons for the desire to be dissolved and to be with Christ (Phil 1:23) is to see him face to face and thoroughly understand the profound and eternal mysteries of his Incarnation, which is by no means the lesser part of beatitude. As Christ himself says to the Father in Saint John's Gospel: *This is eternal life, that they know you, the one true God, and your Son Jesus Christ whom you have sent* (Jn 17:3).

The soul, then, earnestly longs to enter these caverns of Christ in order to be absorbed, transformed, and wholly inebriated in the love of the wisdom of these mysteries, and hide herself in the bosom of the Beloved. In the Song of Songs he invites her to these clefts, saying: *Arise, make haste, my love, my beautiful one, and come into the clefts of the rock and into the cavern of the wall* (Song 2:13–14).

The soul's aim is a love equal to God's. She always desired this equality, naturally and supernaturally, for lovers cannot be satisfied without feeling that they love as much as they are loved. Since the soul sees through her transformation in God in this life that she cannot, even though her love is immense, equal the perfection of God's love for her, she desires the clear transformation of glory in which she will reach this equality.

. . . Besides teaching [the soul] to love purely, freely, and disinterestedly, as he loves us, God makes her love him with the very strength with which he loves her. Transforming her into his love, as we said, he gives her his own strength by which she can love him. As if he were to put an instrument in her hands and show her how it works by operating it jointly with her, he shows her how to love and gives her the ability to do so.

One should not think it impossible that the soul be capable of so sublime an activity as this breathing in God through participation as God breathes in her. For, granted that God favors her by union with the Most Blessed Trinity, in which she becomes deiform and God through participation. . . . God accomplishes this in the soul through communication and participation. This is transformation in the three Persons in power and wisdom and love, and thus the soul is like God through this transformation. He created her in his image and likeness that she might attain such resemblance. . . . No knowledge or power can describe how this happens, unless by explaining how the Son of God attained and merited such a high state for us, the power to be children of God, as Saint John says (Jn 1:12).

— Excerpts from: *The Spiritual Canticle*,
Stanzas 32:6; 37:1, 5; 38:3, 4; 39:4, 5

XXIV

I Went Out from Myself

Communications that are truly from God have this trait: They simultaneously exalt and humble the soul. For on this road, to descend is to ascend and to ascend is to descend, since those who humble themselves are exalted and those who exalt themselves are humbled (Lk 14:11). Besides this (that the virtue of humility exalts), God, in order to exercise the soul in humility, usually makes it ascend by this ladder so that it might descend, and he makes it descend that it might ascend. Accordingly, the Wise Man's words are fulfilled: *Before the soul is*

exalted, it is humbled, and before it is humbled, it is exalted
(Prov 18:12).

This, then, is the disguise the soul says she wore on this secret ladder in the night of faith, and these are its colors. These colors are a most suitable preparation for union of the three faculties (intellect, memory, and will) with God.

Faith darkens and empties the intellect of all its natural understanding and thereby prepares it for union with the divine wisdom.

Hope empties and withdraws the memory from all creature possessions, for as Saint Paul says, hope is for that which is not possessed (Rom 8:24). It withdraws the memory from what can be possessed and fixes it on what it hopes for. Hence only hope in God prepares the memory perfectly for union with him.

Charity also empties and annihilates the affections and appetites of the will of whatever is not God and centers them on him alone. Thus charity prepares the will and unites it with God through love.

Because these virtues have the function of withdrawing the soul from all that is less than God, they consequently have the mission of joining it with God.

Insofar as the soul is buffeted and purged through the war of the dark night in a twofold way (in the sensory and spiritual parts with their senses, faculties, and passions), she also attains a twofold peace and rest in the faculties and appetites of both the sensory and spiritual parts. . . . The sensory and spiritual parts of the soul, in order to go out to the divine union of love, must first be reformed, put in order, and pacified . . .

As soon as these two parts of the soul are wholly at rest and strengthened, together with all the members of the household, the faculties and appetites (also put to sleep and in silence regarding earthly and heavenly things), Divine Wisdom is united with the soul in a new bond of the possession of love. . . . The bride in the Song of Songs explains the same thing when she states that after she passed by those who took away her veil and wounded her, she found him whom her soul loved (Song 3:4; 5:7).

One cannot reach this union without remarkable purity, and this purity is unattainable without vigorous mortification and nakedness regarding all creatures. "Taking off the bride's veil" and "wounding her at night," in her search and desire for her Spouse, signify this denudation and mortification, for she could not put on the new bridal veil without first removing her other one. Persons who refuse to go out at night in search for the Beloved and to divest and mortify their will, but rather seek the Beloved in their own bed and comfort, as did the bride (Song 3:1), will not succeed in finding him. As this soul declares, she found him when she departed in darkness and with longings of love.

—Excerpts from: *The Dark Night*, Book 2:
Chapters 18:2; 21:11; 24:2, 3–4

XXV

The Hidden Indwelling

I should like to persuade spiritual persons that the road leading to God does not entail a multiplicity of considerations, methods, manners and experiences . . . A person makes progress only though imitation of Christ, who is the Way, the Truth, and the Life. No one goes to the Father but through him, as he states of himself in Saint John (Jn 14:6).

It should be known that God dwells secretly in all souls and is hidden in their substance, for otherwise they would not last. . . . Oh, how happy is this soul, which ever experiences God resting and reposing within it! Oh, how fitting it is for it to withdraw from things, flee from business matters, and live in immense tranquility, so that it may not, even with the slightest speck of dust or noise, disturb or trouble its heart where the Beloved dwells.

—Excerpts from: *The Ascent of Mount Carmel*,
Book 2: Chapter 7:8
The Living Flame of Love,
Stanzas 4:14–15

Notes

1. As quoted by Benedict XVI in his general audience of Wednesday, March 17, 2010.

2. Teresa of Ávila, *The Book of Her Foundations*, chapter 3.

3. First stanza of the poem *The Dark Night* by John of the Cross.

4. Aristotle.

5. Aristotle.

BOOKS & MEDIA

A mission of the Daughters of St. Paul

As apostles of Jesus Christ, evangelizing today's world:

We are CALLED to holiness
by God's living Word and Eucharist.

We COMMUNICATE the Gospel message
through our lives and through all
available forms of media.

We SERVE the Church
by responding to the hopes and needs
of all people with the Word of God,
in the spirit of St. Paul.

For more information visit our Web site:
www.pauline.org.

BOOKS & MEDIA

The Daughters of St. Paul operate book and media centers at the following addresses. Visit, call, or write the one nearest you today, or find us on the World Wide Web, www.pauline.org.

CALIFORNIA

3908 Sepulveda Blvd, Culver City, CA 90230	310-397-8676
2650 Broadway Street, Redwood City, CA 94063	650-369-4230
5945 Balboa Avenue, San Diego, CA 92111	858-565-9181

FLORIDA

145 S.W. 107th Avenue, Miami, FL 33174	305-559-6715

HAWAII

1143 Bishop Street, Honolulu, HI 96813	808-521-2731
Neighbor Islands call:	866-521-2731

ILLINOIS

172 North Michigan Avenue, Chicago, IL 60601	312-346-4228

LOUISIANA

4403 Veterans Memorial Blvd, Metairie, LA 70006	504-887-7631

MASSACHUSETTS

885 Providence Hwy, Dedham, MA 02026	781-326-5385

MISSOURI

9804 Watson Road, St. Louis, MO 63126	314-965-3512

NEW YORK

64 W. 38th Street, New York, NY 10018	212-754-1110

PENNSYLVANIA

Philadelphia—relocating	215-676-9494

SOUTH CAROLINA

243 King Street, Charleston, SC 29401	843-577-0175

VIRGINIA

1025 King Street, Alexandria, VA 22314	703-549-3806

CANADA

3022 Dufferin Street, Toronto, ON M6B 3T5	416-781-9131

¡También somos su fuente para libros,
videos y música en español!